Let Go

Christian Poetry

David LaChapelle

28 And we know that in all things God works for the good of those who love him, who have been called according to his purpose. **29** For those God foreknew he also predestined to be conformed to the image of his Son, that he might be the firstborn among many brothers and sisters. **30** And those he predestined, he also called; those he called, he also justified; those he justified, he also glorified.

Romans 8:28-30 (NIV)

POEMS

[3] I thank my God every time I remember you. [4] In all my prayers for all of you, I always pray with joy [5] because of your partnership in the gospel from the first day until now, [6] being confident of this, that he who began a good work in you will carry it on to completion until the day of Christ Jesus.

Philippians 1:3-6 (NIV)

<u>Belonging</u>

God is not responsible

For the pain I feel

He is not in control of suffering

That seems so real

He is a loving Father

In every which way

He opens the skies

To brighten the day

To bring us back home

Into wholeness and liberty

Where we belong

For eternity

<u>Good God</u>

You are not the origins of fear

You are not the cause of my tears

You are not responsible for my pride

You are not the pain in my side

There is only one place to fly

To the open skies

And end the struggle with my flesh

Or at least have a foothold,

On my steps

To live in peace

And be content and happy

I am blessed

Showing

Pain and suffering

May come and go

I do not have to follow its flow

Float down the river of life

Show me what it is all about tonight

So, I can celebrate

And lift my hands to the sky

Where I do not run and hide

From the cares on display

I do not blame you God

For what I have gone through

You are not the cause of distress

So, I can just trust you and rest

That you say who you say you are

To do what you do

To bring me to completion

Loving you

Better Way

God you are not the source of pain

I will not live in vain

There must be a better way

Then to be caught,

In between the day

Liberty is found in your arms

Where you are strong

It is in your hands

You have a plan

I just open my eyes

To see your love in disguise

To not be overtaken by my feelings

Overcome the world with believing

That you died on the cross

To save us all from ourselves

And not be lost

I belong with you

You are my rescue

Trust

You are the man,

With the plan

I must make a stand

To not worry myself to death

Of the uncertainties that life presents

Just focus, that you are working,

Everything for my good

To restore me to who.

I am meant to be

And everything I should see

In this life and beyond

To make your love known,

To those who are outside,

Trying to run and hide

I have been there before

So, I know the score

Plea

I do not blame you for,

the pressures and stressors

Feelings used to open and close the doors

They come and go no more

There is a watch over my soul

A good Shepard protecting my steps

To be receptive to His plan

To be a better man

And know what life is about

And why I am here

Struggling without

I have you

And that is all I need to do

You hear my plea

Eternity

Game

God is not in control of my pain

It is a plain game that is lame

That can only be won

In the spirit of the sun

It cannot be any clearer than that

Deep down inside

I look up

Where freedom is found in the fight

Chaos is the norm

These are settling a form

Like it is meant to be

We will wait and see

For the promises to come to thee

Higher Way

I am willing to wait

To provide for my needs

While I let go

Into the unknown

Trusting in you Lord

Higher than the norm,

And values I have been taught,

That are not from above

To a better place

That does not come up short

It is a journey

You are with me

Every step of the way

Along for the ride

You are by my side

You loved me first

I love in return

A special day,

It will be

When I am all yours

In your loving arms

Forevermore

Game II

It is a lame game plain to play

Where there is only one winner

The saint and the sinner

Who are one in the sun

Like a tropical fruit: Mango and Coconuts

Ripe for the final days

Where we belong

Come as you are

And end the striving to make ourselves known

We will be in your loving arms

Forevermore

Bloom

The consequences are hidden,

in the believer

To seal the deal for real

That we are looking for a country

Where we will be ripe and ready,

With zeal

To live beyond anything. we can imagine

This life has its classrooms

Lessons to learn to develop in the storm

To be solid and sure

In the rock and in form

Response

I prayed for deliverance

You heard me calling you

You answered a few moments later

Now the Pharisee is at the altar

With my worship and praise

Trying to complete the sprit in the flesh

I have come back to you full circle

To see if you are near

To know I am not forgotten

And you will hear my plea

Resting

I lay down my will again

For the second time in the daylight

I feel discontent

So, I know am straying,

off the concourse of faith

That we need to get back to you

And get away from these feeling of due

To be purposeful once again

And know I am in your loving care

I do not know what to do

Just trust in you

To show me the way,

to a better day,

to where I do not run and hide

and stray

<u>Fighting</u>

My way is in play

Trying to be in charge

I need a discharge

To be free from myself

And stride of this life

To be content again

And feel known and secure

I do not want to be in control

Bring me back to you Lord

I am all yours

No Rights

Pain comes and goes

Putting on a show

To blow,

Its horns,

Of discomfort to tow

I do not want to be a defendant in a case

You will help me find my place

I surrender my rights

For something better

Rescue me Lord from myself

I need a commendation letter of approval

To save my feathers

Forever

<u>Breaking</u>

Letting go

Is like breaking a dam

Releasing the hinderances

That were not made to stand

Allowing the river of life

To flow within me

Opportunities

Opening me up

Discoveries

Where I will be fully known

In His Grace

Set before me

This is love

Fully blossoming

Good Order

God is responsible for the message

Not the trials and lies

He is responsible for my files

That stack up against His love

Being organized from above

To send a good report in

That everything is fine within

To lead me to the open fields

Where the sun has a shield

And blossom

In its light

And make everything alright

<u>Shaping</u>

You stretched me out

Discovering my ways

You spin me round

Molding me like clay

I am seeing who I am

A vessel of your love

Made more like you

Each and everyday

Blessings from above

Depending on you

Freedom speaks

You belong to me

Relaxation

Trick or treat

Let have a feast

I am hungry for more

Show me the open door

Where freedom is found

And I can make all the sound I want

Fully completely

Away from the snares of the enemy

And let my hair down

And relax for eternity

Due Season

I have come to the end

Of struggling within

To claim His promises

To win over sin

Full fruition

Due season

Giving me hope

A new beginning

For believing

In something greater than me

Humbling myself,

Before you Lord

Secret

You are the light

That makes everything alright

The day bright

To give me sight

So, I can fight another day

To what is right

Fly the banner of love

That you have redeemed mankind,

from above

So, save me first Lord

I promise I will not tell

It is our secret

Shhhh!

Staying

God is good

He is not the cause of trials and hurts

I had to take ownership of my feelings

Not make an identity out of my pleading

He will rescue me from myself

If I stay in His loving arms

And trust in His Grace

The person of Jesus

His name above every other name

Who better to know

To do what He promised

In His Word

Made flesh in this world

To show us an example

Of His love

To know the way

To make it back home

On that Glorious day

When we will be made

In His image

For eternity

<u>Lifted</u>

A cloud has lifted

The ambers smolder

Catch a breath

What a relief,

From the stress

The unknown pressure

There is no way to measure

Its purpose known to God

I just know how to cope

It is getting old

Bring me back into the fold

I have been told

Escape

The burden has passed through the skies

All the trials and lies

Peace does not evade

Contentment is a creative escape

To not run and hide

Just bide my time for the ride

Wait for the morning light to arrive

Change my nights to days

Be productive in the sun,

And have some fun in the shade

Moving

When you rescued me Lord

I wanted to make an altar

A marker to stop and gaze upon

You would not let me camp there

You have other plans for me

To take me further than I was willing to go

Develop in your likeness

To bring others to wholeness

To your light and fullness

To save the day for a better way

Need

I do not have what it takes

To live the impossible Christian life

To have faith

For the times we are in

I need a Savior that knows me within

To show me the way

To keep me on course

Not lose hope

He will provide

When I face the tides

No Rest

I do not know what to believe

I am losing my faith

I am losing myself in the race

The story does not end there

We are soon going to set sails

In paradise forevermore

Leave everything behind

What a score

It will be fine

The unknown to wrestle with

We are human

There is no rest

Till He calls us home

We will know what it is to be known

The Blues

The clouds lifted

They pass by with the breeze

Cannot control the weather

I am displeased

I want to feel good all the time

That is not reality

In this fallen world

That is why I need the Lord

To take me through

The Blues

Content

I do not deserve anything

Whatever the Lord provides

Is enough

God is a God of infinite love,

gentleness and compassion

He knows my story,

from beginning to end

There is no surprising Him

So, I humble myself before Jesus,

And He has opened the door,

To peace and offerings and blessings

Resting in His awesome bosom

All the rest of my days

<u>Not Me</u>

God knows me inside out

He is aware of what it takes,

To bring me to the end of myself

I have been pouring out,

my heart in disbelief for quite sometime

Faith in God,

As He empties me,

of what is not from Him

and undesirable

To make me whole and complete

Lacking no good things

Wanting nothing but peace

<u>Winning</u>

The day finally arrived
Through praying and keeping time
That I came to the end of myself
Of struggling to have my way
Surrendering control
Humbling my soul before the Lord

I thought I needed what I lost
Now my self-entitlement attitude
Is released played a big part
A gain for Christ
I feel lighter than before
More of Him that is for sure
I am winning
Who is keeping score

Found

Always wanting more

Never satisfied

Never enough

No matter what it was

I wanted freedom from Jesus

He would not let me go

The Lord knew me better

He was not keeping score

One thing to the next

Always something put on me

I could not rest

A discourse kept me running around

An obstacle course making me sick

I gave up one day

He found me

Anticipation

The time has come;

To lay it all down;

To give up my rights,

From wearing a frown

Surrender control

I am more open than before

Not vulnerable as I thought,

protected and loved ever more

It was all an illusion

That my ego portrayed

That I needed it to be kept at bay

Now I am free in harmony

With the one who knows me

He will have all of me in due time

Cannot wait for the day

When everything will be fine

Hooray!

Coming Round

The Lord knows best

He is hard to trust,

because of my flesh

Born into this fallen world,

my ego and hurt around hurled

Insults at God

That He does not know,

what is going on

Forgiveness takes sometime

When pain invades and,

screams for attention

Here I am please

Focus on God

And his best intentions

Will bring you to where you,

were meant to be

The end of yourself

Living in harmony

Relief

The fight within,

I could not win

The veil over my eyes,

had to rescind

To bring me to a place

Where my heart can groove

To His heartbeat

Nothing to prove

To the open door,

I walked on through

The darkness left,

without saying boo

It caused me so much pain

It had no substance

Just plain vain

It was using me for its purpose

Drawing the life out of me

I could not refuse it

Had to forgive,

to let it go

Now I am on my way,

to your love

Race

It was early May

God spoke to my heart

In the late

He said to me

You are full of yourself

You deserve nothing

He opened a door

The darkness disappeared in its form

Its power and threats,

were just a phantom of care

The work is done

It is time to have fun

Freedom was always around the corner

Could not steer the wheel,

To move forward

Stuck in neutral

Sometimes going in reverse

It was a struggle,

I never thought to lose

I could not win the race

Was deluded in every case

The Lord knows what to do

To bring me to end of my cool

Where life begins now

I made it this far

I am happy

Wow!

Confused

Always wanting more

Never satisfied with the score

Doubting God's provision and vision

Dismantling my defences

Till I come forth

To the suffering caused by me

I was playing God

How can that be?

Unable to perform

I did not know it

Until I was reformed

The Lord brought me through it

I was born with a fallen nature

It is not my fault

I am human

ABOUT THE AUTHOR

David LaChapelle is a born-again Christian since the year 2000. David has earned himself two Computer Technical Diplomas from Seneca College in Toronto, Canada in 1994 and 1996. He graduated with a Psychology degree in 2011 from Trent University in Peterborough, Canada where he now calls home. David lives a quiet life and enjoys writing and being an author. He is proud of his works and hopes it will bring him recognition in this life and rewards hereafter. David is a firm believer in reading the Word of God and the power of prayer and wishes the best for all humanity awaiting the Lord's return.

OTHER BOOKS BY DAVID LACHAPELLE

David's Adventure with Schizophrenia: My Road to Recovery

David's Journey with Schizophrenia: Insight into Recovery

David's Victory Thru Schizophrenia: Healing Awareness

David's Poems: A Poetry Collection

1000 Canadian Expressions and Meanings: EH!

Freedom in Jesus

Canadian Slang Sayings and Meanings: Eh!

The Biggest Collection of Canadian Slang: Eh!

Healing Hidden Emotions for Believers

Breaking Clouds: Christian Poetry

Walking Light: Christian Poetry

All books and e-books available at Amazon

Manufactured by Amazon.ca
Bolton, ON